Classical

Isabelle Rieger

BookLeaf Publishing

India | USA | UK

Presentation by *BookLeaf Publishing*

Web: www.bookleafpub.com

E-mail: info@bookleafpub.com

ISBN: 9789357444217

First edition 2022

DEDICATION

This book is dedicated to my brother, Harry.

There is no more prominent figure entwined in my life than you. You are larger than life in both personality and kindness, with talent and self-belief to back you. Whilst I acknowledge that you do not voluntarily read poetry, my love for you is unconditional. I can find no better way to express that than to leave it here in ink for the rest of time. This will outlast you and me, even then there will be proof of just how loved you are. I am overjoyed that you are here with me.

CONTENTS

Stasis

There is a fine line between empty and worn in
used and weathered but not crumbling
A moment when time progresses but does not
degrade
The moment a droplet hits the paper
it sits there
throwing light
a beautiful shape
There is that moment just as it sinks in
before you have realised the damage

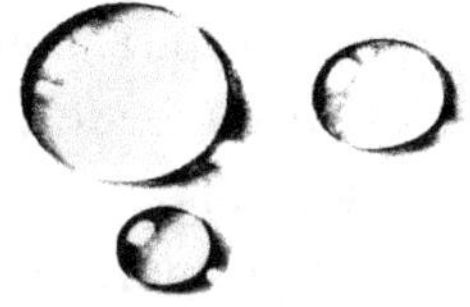

Art Nouveau

She was the modernista of Stile Floreal
A botanical study of the Belle Epoque
A product of the luminaries' curiosity

Woven into the fabric of her dress
Are the skeletons of deep-sea organisms
a membrane of concentric shapes
folds: the aligning of surfaces
kissing with anxious eroticism

The ceramic shards of her visage
knit into oriental emotions
Expressions cloaked in her hair
tendrils of India ink illustrations
infused with the scent of geranium and rosewood

Electric femininity carves a spiral path to her centre
where incandescence waits to be released
on the breath of an elated lung
The last gasps of a citrus perfume muffled underground
Her coffin is made of ice and burning sage

She evocatively blooms in the darkness
The stark sexuality of knotted bodies
rippling patterns in shadowy images
evaporate into the crowd
Now only remembered by Le Metro signs

The Watchmaker

In the glass garden of minutes
He was the maestro of the sun
An attentive curator of the moon

His face a delicate construction
of silver wrinkles and tidal currents
which bump into the turret of his nose
His eyes, the colour of a flooded church
His lips, a palace destroyed

His hair is forged of perforated gold
moulded into longitudinal tresses
and gilded with white alloy as age settles in.
A tiny forgotten hammer nestles
behind his delicate ears

Under the scrutiny of a curious lantern
his graceful hands weave
French roses into iron wheels
German music into an engine and
Spring into a helix which will never change season

He turns the key by half a degree
as the memoirs of astronomers set on fire
Eternity bucks in his silken hands
coiling into the chamber of his magnetic palms
gently bound in diamonds and handed to the King

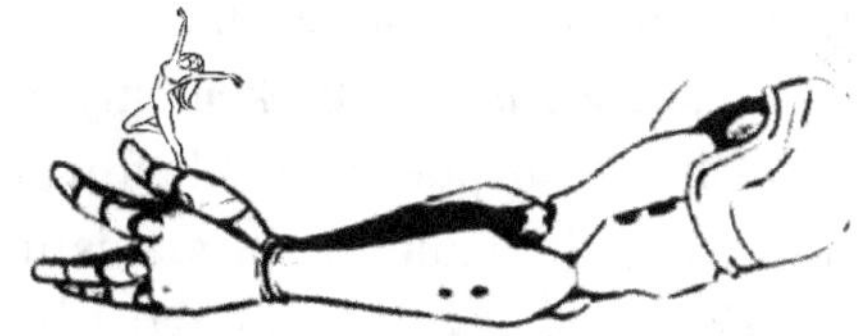

Masterpiece in Retrograde

Dusk nights upon dreary bushfires. I wait holding a crystal glass, filled two thirds the colour of the sky. Your charcoal fingers knock on the door, leaving ash on oak. Avant-garde Miscreant is how you signed your works. My house is now a gilded frame. The floor of sketches, the walls of colour theory, the rafters made of pencil lead. Your hard lines, thick curves and feathered edges transpose onto flesh, as I drag my limbs. Tumbling onto an empty landscape, the silence unites, broken only by the windchimes I hung outside the kitchen window when I was five. The gaunt earth yields to the horizon, which bends like a broken wrist. To the bronze ballet of childhood phantoms, I wait. The violent clouds roll in, the dark honey colour of hope. Thunder breaks with the scent of vanilla.

Concrete Hinterland

In our concrete hinterland
baby's breath blooms from the pallid ground
        tiny supernovas
from a cosmos ground down with mortar and
pestle

A deep honeysuckle hum emerges
        These places are   split
As thunderclouds of dark rose chiffon
Blanket our dissolving city
      drip   drip   drop
a newsstand of rotting paper and empty cigarette
lighters
        drip   drip   crack
us citizens of nowhere

We waged war,   rouge scullery
against the bozos

     drip-drip-teardrop
Lovers are sacred
        Sunspots on your gunmetal cheeks

Eternity and Time

I
The moon in a tea cosy
    twinkles at half mast
our bones and eyes
    a sprinkle of stardust on the canvas of time
She dances from swell to swell
    swaying from the rigging
A tinkling of the whales' windchimes.
The blue water of dawn filled the room

II
Lost ideas and blank books;
        papier mâché coffins
Where did eternity go?
    I've come back with the inability
    to manage Time
The moon is running late
    he has heard from neither sister

III
I found Time
    she was nestled away
warming her hands
    on the ocean's depths
Eternity's glass eyes pass us by
    Searching for a place to settle
But Time, she wants to stay still
    Just for a few minutes longer

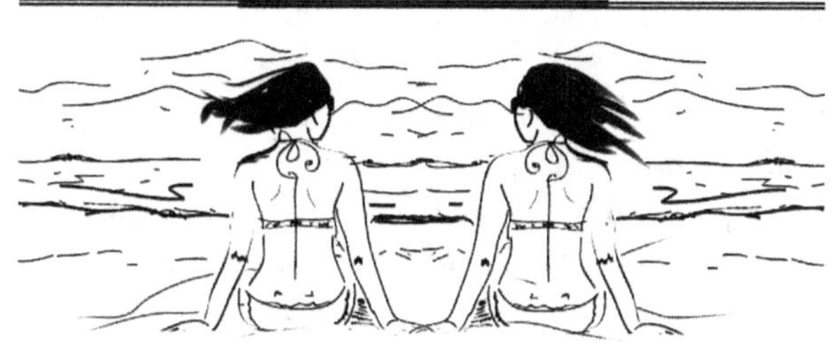

California Dreaming

Black coffee and beached submarines in the dead of night
illuminated by neon cigars and the collective American
subconscious.
You're safe. The late-night highways echo with jazz, and our
aluminum roadster.
Deserted theaters, a transient hotel, dusty brothels and an
indistinct calm
nothing but my baroque California girl and the steering wheel.
Screaming in sheer joy as we pass the architecture of broken
dreams
fission, concrete, plaster and lathing. Our semiotic ghosts kill
the headlights.
We're translucent at this wavelength. finite.
The sundial chimes as your amphetamine tears drop
and our lopsided orbital in twilight
                Nothing but chrome cigarette butts.

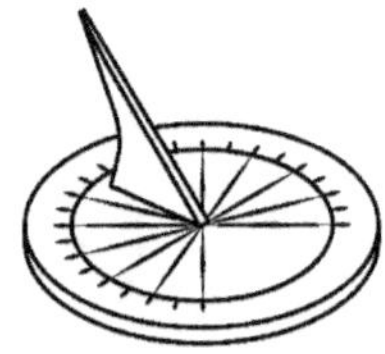

Japanese Jazz

Mid-mornings to slow jazz and cicadas
The same song plays on repeat
An artist rests under an eastern shade
with his radio, contemplating an earthquake
and what key it would play the sax in

In an underground club
an anxious phantom makes sandwiches
for all the missing cats in Kobe
who fell down a dry well
They are tough and a little punk

A Tokyo child commutes to the netherworld
for his night job at a stationary store
The adjacent train carriage
spirits are dressed in their finest paintings
for the Kyoto Opera

A yellow jumper against a concrete playground
A musician lies on her back
mapping connections between tsunamis
and traditional Japanese literature
as the Osaka underworld tenderly swallows her
whole

Shipwreck

Driftwood ribs turned over in her sleep
the ship keens under the weight of evening
creaking gently about the sand in her stomach
Her bones so bare not even the gulls have nested
in her slowly disintegrating body

As my toes sink into the shell-grit by the water
a wave unearths timbers that must belong to her brother
The galaxies overhead hide behind the clouds
instead of looking at what is forgotten
With seaweed stuck between his oak teeth, I leave him.

Docked by the pier in a composed old lady
wearing a balustrade from decades prior
She radiates peace, sails folded as a shawl for the night
Her hull scrubbed clean and anchor firm
I bid her goodnight and wonder on.

A teakwood gentleman is gazing at the stars
he sits low in the water as barnacles drag him down
He bares scars from the reef and encounters with the seas
He is not much longer for this harbour
but an elderly albatross stays by his side

At the end of the pier there is the ocean
and a little boat belonging to me
I hear the lady murmur in her sleep
of beautiful places and worlds
which only the brave will ever see

Eroding Vignettes

Waves retreating
    Worn down sandstone
Stretch marks
    Vinegar disease of film
Burnt out candles
    Split ends in the sink
Tarnished silver spoons
    Mildew on shower ceilings
Holes worn in the flyscreen
    Tobacco stained sheets

Paralian

15

I went to the ocean
but it was out to lunch.

A sign left
and the sea plain

Yellow railroad sleepers
buried in the sand

Storm washed Blue
A slow train's coming

Express route to Neptune

Poolside

cracked pavement filled with moss
wildflowers
and forget me nots

Night Blues

Fibre optics in the wind
reflect on a nocturnal sea
robin's eggs rest in the fuse box while
midnight's seafoam laps against the telephone
poles

Sealight

A flame flickers in a seashell: candles on the
shoreline,
carving paths into the limestone cliffs
and illuminating bracken
as it stoops over in the wind

Sepia

Your thoughts
are all sharp angles
        and deep water

Alongside a train of which you have lost

And in the trainyard lies a rotting boat
did the ocean once reach here?

To my Heart,

In Time
      perhaps
this light will fade
the friction of our crash
will dissipate
and yet
      perhaps
            In Time
we will continue to circle here
dimmed and forgotten
but made of just the same particles
as before.

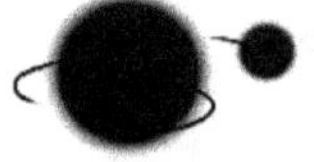

Autumn Leaves

Winter breathes deeply
   As she begins to rouse
Autumn packs his bags
   Stripping the room bare
He pecks his lover's cheek
   Leaving before she is awake

The Pianist

He makes music with the space
        between his fingers
The gap between Mercury
        and Venus
carries the same lilting melody

His minims dance on the page
        writing the same song
that a black hole sings
        as it swallows the stars
A cosmic symphony penned on a paper sky

His muscles stretch to reach notes
        as time extends its branches
to gently push at
        the edges of the universe
His small fingers the size of space

ACKNOWLEDGEMENT

I cannot go without acknowledging the people in my past and present who have taught me and facilitated my independence.

To my parents, the greatest thanks for instilling in me a thirst for knowledge, and drive to create and explore. I know without a doubt that I am loved and supported, and for that, I am beyond grateful.

To my teachers, from school to university, the calibre and dedication of this wonderful group of people inspire me and give me an enthusiasm for a literary life.

And not least to my friends. To those who have made me laugh, and held me while I cried, you give me direction and meaning. A special mention must go to my personal Mad Hatter, for always being my accomplice, as I am sure you will continue to be for decades more.

www.ingramcontent.com/pod-product-compliance
Lightning Source LLC
LaVergne TN
LVHW021357200726